Copyright © 2015 Daniel R. Ford,

All rights reserved

No part of this publication may be reproduced in any form by any means known now and of technology known in the future, stored in a retrieval system, or transmitted in any form or by any means, electronic, mechanical, photocopying, recording, or otherwise without written permission of the publisher and the author.

Green Seahorse Media LLC

2621 Elson Green Ave

Va. Beach Va., 23456

ISBN 978-0-985-52954-3

Library of Congress Control Number:

2015906024

Illustrations in this book were created using colored pencils.

Illustrated by Tatiana Retter

This book is in memory of
Kamalani Anuhea Kalama,
honoring her
through art and poetry.

Giving the glory to God for the life
Kamalani shared with friends and
family.

We also honor her parents,
Jackie and Jerry,
And the Kalama Ohana.

Both Jackie and Jerry
are advocates of
and educators for MADD.

About the Author

Daniel R. Ford, a graduate of Longwood College (now Longwood University) has written three rhyming children's picture books designed to educate children and their families about sustainability for the aquatic environment. His hopes are to inspire readers to become active stewards and proponents for our waterways. His lifelong love of the water makes this a natural choice for his message. Daniel lives in Virginia Beach with his family.

About the Illustrator

Tatiana Retter, originally from Russia, graduated with a Master's degree in Illustration and Graphics from the Moscow Printing Academy before moving to the United States. A mother of three, the Virginia Beach resident founded the Magic of Art Studio to share her many artistic talents and love of art in educating others.
Among her favorite pursuits is illustrating books, especially children's books.

Near a stretch of atolls
By the Hawaiian Islands,
Lives Mermaid Kamalani
And some friends who are stylin'.

Mermaid Kamalani
Is filled with love from within,
She has dark almond eyes
And a gorgeous tailfin.

She cares for the creatures
In the water and on land,
She likes hanging loose
Near the shore on the sand.

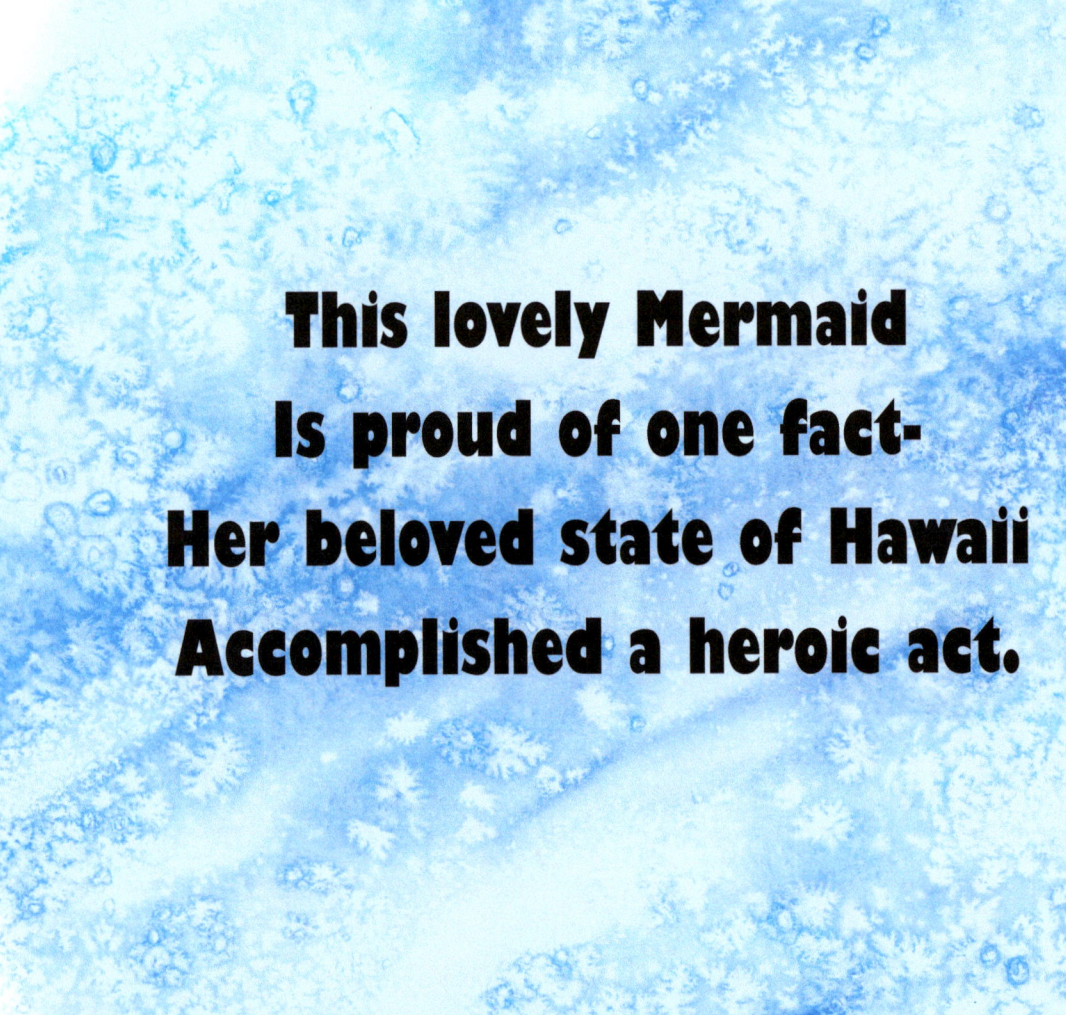

**This lovely Mermaid
Is proud of one fact-
Her beloved state of Hawaii
Accomplished a heroic act.**

They signed into law
A preventive measure,
To ban plastic bags
And to protect Mother Nature!

Her friends are green sea turtles
Strong and brave are they,
Swimming all the oceans
For work and for play.

Early one morning
When the weather was fine,
The trio was surfing
The waves at Pipeline.

When on the horizon
They spot a sea of debris,
Caused by a powerful earthquake
And giant tsunamis.

There's paper, there's plastic,
oil drums, and cans of gas.
There's fishing nets and lumber-
All types of harmful trash!

The turtles love their ocean
And are first in their class,
One thing they don't like-
They don't like trash!

Mermaid Kamalani
With her sea turtle friends,
Paddle the Molokai channel
From the start to the end.

Between Lanai and Molokai

Are favorite social grounds,

Where whales, sharks, manta rays,

And the largest fish can be found.

Jumping on an outrigger canoe

Mermaid Kamalani takes a ride,

Heading towards the shores of Maui

With the sea turtles by her side.

Maui is the second largest island

Where warm waters are alluring,

For migrating humpback whales

And whale watchers who are touring.

Windsurfing to Kauai
On a blustery day,
Mermaid Kamalani gets air
While the pair likes to play.

Kauai is the oldest island

Of the main Hawaiian chain,

One of the wettest places on earth

With 400 inches of yearly rain.

This thick, sweet syrup

Had seeped into the bay,

Harming its inhabitants

Who couldn't get out of the way.

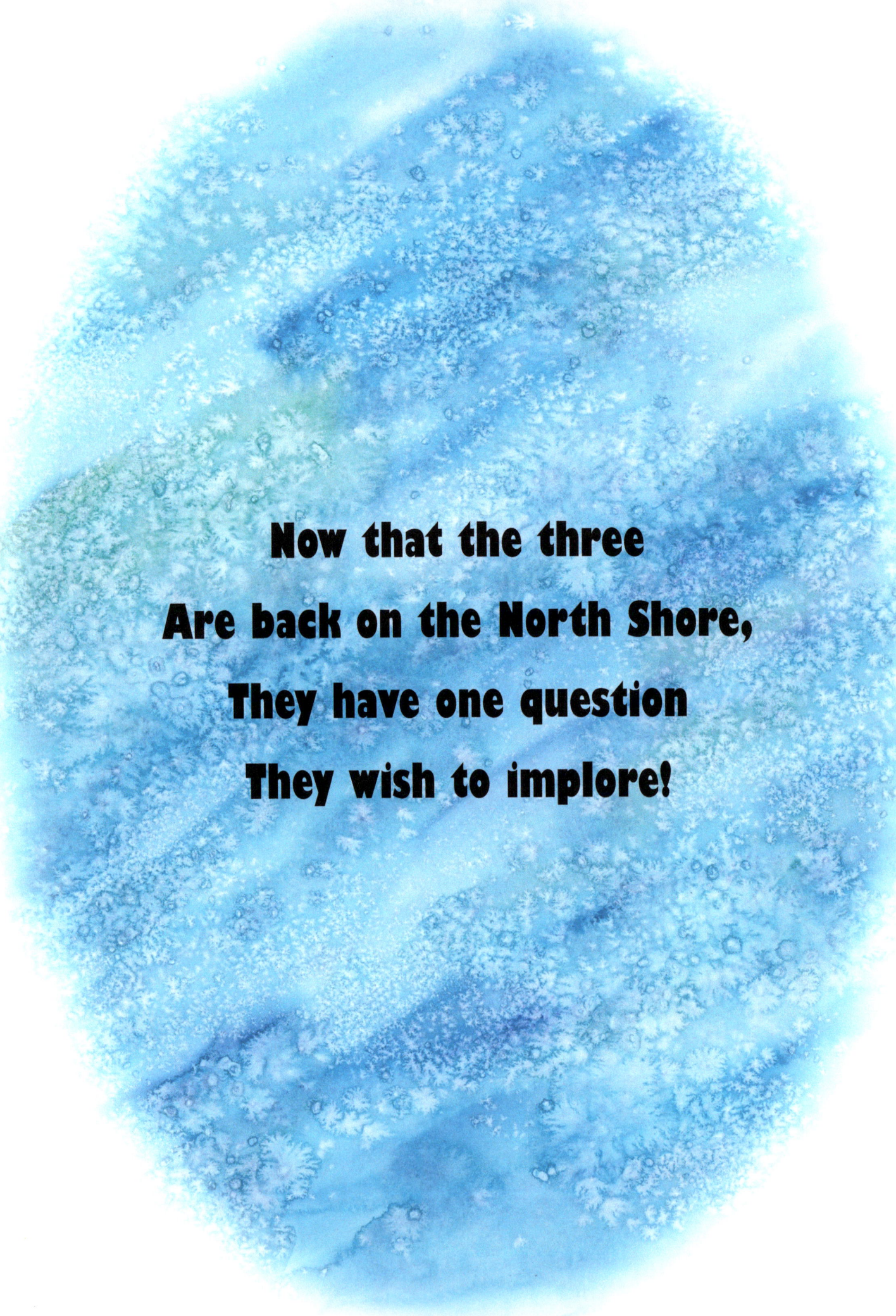

Now that the three
Are back on the North Shore,
They have one question
They wish to implore!

What can we all do
To help clean our seas?
Any suggestions?
If so, tell me please!

GLOSSARY

Atoll- A ring-shaped reef or island formed by coral that surrounds a lagoon.

Earthquake- An event which occurs along cracks in the Earth's surface resulting in sudden rolling or shaking movement.

Green Sea Turtles- A large sea turtle that can average between 200 and 400 pounds. Green sea turtles played a large role in Polynesian and Micronesian cultures.

Hawaii- Became the 50th state of United States on August 21st, 1959. The capital is Honolulu and it is the only state that is totally made up of islands.

Hawaiian Monk Seals- The Hawaiian monk seals entire range is within U.S. waters and is one of the rarest of marine mammals in the world.

Humpback Whale- Can grow to be more than 50 feet in length and weigh over seventy thousand pounds. They migrate 16,000 miles a year to breed and give birth typically in the tropical or subtropical waters. One of their favorite social grounds is located in Hawaii.

North Shore- An area located on the island of Oahu known for epic surfing spots including Waimea Bay, Sunset Beach, and Banzai Pipeline.

Tsunami– These are waves produced by an earthquake or underwater landslides. They can reach speeds up to 600 miles per hour and reach heights over 100 feet. Waves between 10 to 20 feet can be very dangerous and destructive.

Volcanoes– They tend to occur along the edges of tectonic plates and contain lava and molten rock. There are four types of volcanoes: cinder cones, lava domes, composite and shield volcanoes. There are over 1500 active volcanoes on our planet.

To my Wife
Whose Heart flows with passion,
Whose Soul is gentle and kind,
Whose Wisdom provides great insight,
And to our Love-
Which dwells along the 8th wavelength!

Kamalani Anuhea Kalama was born on
August 9, 1999 in Kailua, Oahu, Hawaii.
She was a student at Kainalu Elementary School
and went on to Kailua Intermediate
School where she was a leader to all.
She was a mentor, a peer educator,
an advocate, and a friend.
She encouraged positive relationships
with everyone.
Kamalani was also an athlete enjoying hiking, soccer,
volleyball, and, most especially, ocean sports.
Through her participation on the Kailua Canoe Club,
Kamalani brought her strong connection to the
ocean and her inspirational skills together. She encouraged her teammates during practices and races
to never give up. Kamalani's love for the ocean was
more than just a paddle in the water;
She strived for teamwork, safety, and conservation of
the aina (land) and the kai (water).
The Kalama family has a strong history in the
paddling community and Kamalani perpetuated this.

Malama pono a hui hou.

"Take care, until we meet again sweet angel."

With Love,
Mom and Dad